NEAR TO GOD

A DEVOTIONAL BIBLE STUDY OF GOD'S CHARACTER IN OUR SUFFERING

LAURI A. HOGLE, PHD

CONTENTS

Trade paperback ISBN: 979-8-9855573-0-5
ePub ISBN: 979-8-9855573-1-2

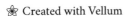 Created with Vellum

As J. S. Bach inscribed on his notated manuscripts, I praise the Lord with "Soli Deo Gloria." It is for God's glory that this book exists, by His grace.

I am forever thankful for my dear husband Paul, my children, church friends, readers who have become new friends, and sister authors who have urged me to share.

To the pastors and Bible teachers who have been God's gift of grace to me, thank you.

"To the only wise God be glory forevermore through Jesus Christ! Amen" (Rom. 16:27).

SDG

INTRODUCTION

I was 25. Being a new mother was the moment I'd been waiting for! My joy overflowed into loving baby and husband and music work.

Two months later, the pain began. I started dropping things and it felt like I had the flu, all the time. My health traveled up and down (with no diagnosis) over the next five years. Despite chronic symptoms and punctuating emergencies, we had twins, I taught piano, and served as a church music director, choir director, and organist. Over the next three years, symptoms progressed to collapsing organ systems, disability, and continual crisis. Hospitals, ambulances, church meal trains, and lament engulfed our life.

In desperate agony, I sought the Lord in His Word. So patiently, God taught me who He is and how deeply He loved me as I wrestled with "why?" and prayed "help me." The Lord lavished me with a grace-filled daily plan — "The LORD is my strength and my shield; in him my heart trusts, and I am helped; my heart exults, and with my song I give thanks to him" (Ps. 28:7). He beckoned me to trust who His Word says He is, by thanking Him in song.

When my doctor told me I needed to prepare to die, still with no diagnosis or working treatment, we called upon the elders of our church, obeying James 5. The very week they prayed around my wheelchair, the Lord intervened. By cascading works of His providence and grace, His miraculous and quick diagnosis brought me to a healing brain surgery after eight years of illness! I lived to raise my daughters, celebrate 34 years (so far) of marriage to my dear husband, and to love five grandbabies (so far)! To God be the glory!

In my pain, I needed to better understand what the Bible says is true about God. The enemy constantly attacked me with lies about the Lord, as I suffered. Who is God? What is He like? What is the essence or character of God? How does this intersect with my suffering? Is He near to me in my agony? How can I endure suffering with faith, hope, peace, and joy? How can knowing God's character offer me hope?

I pray this book will help you draw near to God as you answer these questions, through Scripture, prayer, and song. If you're using an E-book, grab your journaling tools and a Bible as you enter His presence in prayer. May God enfold you in His loving arms, sister in Christ.

DAY 1: LOVE

$\mathcal{I}$n the heavy weight of ongoing suffering, it's so easy to doubt God's love for us. It's an age-old question, deriving from the Genesis 3 fall with Satan's hiss, "Did God actually say?"

God's Word is filled with honest laments, words of agony-prayers of His suffering children. In all but one (Ps. 88), they turn around into praise of who God says He is. How?

They often praise God for His love, a defining love unique to only God, a kind that we can't adequately translate from the Hebrew *hesed*.

It's loving-kindness, steadfast, enduring, unfailing, covenant, loyal, merciful, compassionate, faithful, unconditional, grace-filled, just, righteous, eternal, never-ending love. We don't even have words for God's *hesed* love, but it encompasses God in His fundamental essence.

I'm suffering, "but I have trusted in your steadfast love; my heart shall rejoice in your salvation" (Ps. 13:5). I'm suffering, "but this I call to mind, and therefore I have hope: The steadfast love of the LORD never ceases" (Lam. 3:21-22).

Are you like me? I need constant, daily reminders. "Let me hear in the morning of your steadfast love" (Ps. 143:8).

As we read of His *hesed* love in the Old Testament laments, we now see it displayed on the cross. Beloved in Christ, Jesus is how we know

1

His love still endures for us as we suffer. Because God brought you into a covenantal relationship with Jesus, God's *hesed* love for you...is as Your Father.

What do you re-discover about His love for you in these verses?

ROMANS 5:8

ROMANS 8:35-39

I JOHN 4:9-10

ISAIAH 54:10

My prayer-song to You, loving Father

IN MY SUFFERING, YOU SAY THIS IS TRUE:

SO, IN MY SUFFERING, I PRAISE YOU BECAUSE:

IN MY SUFFERING, PLEASE HELP ME WITH:

INTO MY SUFFERING, I'LL SING THESE SONGS FROM MY PLAYLIST TO YOU TODAY:

Jesus loves me, this I know,
for the Bible tells me so...
Yes, Jesus loves me!
The Bible tells me so.

("JESUS LOVES ME," WARNER, A. B., *1859*)

♪ ♪ ♪

What wondrous love is this
that caused the Lord of bliss
to bear the dreadful curse for my soul, for my soul,
to bear the dreadful curse for my soul!

("WHAT WONDROUS LOVE IS THIS," AMERICAN FOLK HYMN, *1835*)

♪ ♪ ♪

Loved with everlasting love,
drawn by grace that love to know,
Spirit sent from Christ above,
thou dost witness it is so,
O this full and precious peace
from his presence all divine;
In a love that cannot cease,
I am his and he is mine.

Taste the goodness of the Lord:
welcomed home to his embrace,
all his love, as blood outpoured,
seals the pardon of his grace.
Can I doubt his love for me,
when I trace that love's design?
By the cross of Calvary
I am his and he is mine.

("LOVED WITH EVERLASTING LOVE," ROBINSON, G. W., *1890*)

DAY 2: GLORIOUS

*W*hen darkness and ugly infiltrate our thoughts in suffering, we grasp for light and beauty. Can you see anything glorious in nature today? "The heavens declare the glory of God, and the sky above proclaims his handiwork" (Ps. 19:1).

Because He is majestically glorious, beautiful, and radiant, God's created work shines His glory. "For by him all things were created, in heaven and on earth, visible and invisible, whether thrones or dominions or rulers or authorities—all things were created through him and for him" (Col. 1:16).

God's brightness is dazzling (Lk. 9:29-31) like a devouring fire cloud (Ex. 24:16-17). One day, there'll be no need of sun or moon because God's glory will light up the entire new heaven and earth (Rev. 21:22-25). God's eternal and weighty glory is so bright, it was dangerous for Moses to see directly (Ex. 33:20-23). Simply being in the presence of God's glory caused his skin to glow (Ex. 34:29-35).

In today's suffering, do you ache to see God's glory and beauty? (Ex. 33:18; Ps. 27:4). Do you desire His light?

"For God, who said, 'Let light shine out of darkness,' has shone in our hearts to give the light of the knowledge of the glory of God *in the face of Jesus Christ*" (2 Cor. 4:6, emphasis added). We see His glory in

Jesus, God who's always with us by His indwelling Spirit. So, how does God's glory affect you in today's suffering?

What do you re-discover about His glory in these verses?

Isaiah 6:1-7

Isaiah 43:7

2 Corinthians 3:13-18

Psalm 29:2

Romans 11:36

My prayer-song to You, glorious Father

In my suffering, You say this is true:

So, in my suffering, I praise You because:

In my suffering, please help me with:

Into my suffering, I'll sing these songs from my playlist to You today:

Glory be to the Father,
and to the Son,
and to the Holy Ghost;
As it was in the beginning,
is now, and ever shall be,
world without end. Amen, amen.

("GLORIA PATRI," 2ND CENTURY)

♪ ♪ ♪

Fairest Lord Jesus, Ruler of all nature,
Son of God and Son of Man!
Thee will I cherish, thee will I honor,
Thou, my soul's glory, joy, and crown.

Fair are the meadows, fair are the woodlands,
Robed in the blooming garb of spring:
Jesus is fairer, Jesus is purer,
Who makes the woeful heart to sing.

Fair is the sunshine, fair is the moonlight,
And all the twinkling, starry host:
Jesus shines brighter, Jesus shines purer
Than all the angels heav'n can boast.

Beautiful Savior! Lord of the nations!
Son of God and Son of Man!
Glory and honor, praise, adoration,
Now and for evermore be thine.

("FAIREST LORD JESUS," MÜNSTER GESANGBUCH, 1677)

DAY 3: SOVEREIGN

"*W*hat if thoughts" jab our souls as we suffer. We try to bravely face unknowns, constantly planning for future challenges. It's exhausting because suffering feels scary. Suffering can produce fear when we think about possible outcomes. Anxiety looms in a dark cloud.

But Who holds every detail of the future? Every outcome? The Lord, Adonai, supremely in control, and fully self-sufficient. He is sovereign. His sovereignty soothes our fears and brings peace about "what if."

"Are not two sparrows sold for a penny? And not one of them will fall to the ground apart from your Father. But even the hairs of your head are all numbered. Fear not, therefore; you are of more value than many sparrows" (Mt. 10:29-31).

The panicked disciples shook Jesus awake when it seemed that a sudden storm would kill them all, accusing Him, "Do you not care that we are perishing?" (Mk. 4:38). With His answer, Jesus gently questions us too: "Why are you so afraid?" (v. 40). The wind and the sea calmed by His commanding word (vv. 39-41). The storms submitted to the sovereign authority of the One who wisely and lovingly controls all things (Job 38-41) and holds all things together (Col. 1:17).

Immeasurable peace floods my heart when the Creator reminds me of His sovereign control over sparrows and storms in the universe He powerfully sustains. Because He then controls the storms of my personal suffering. I can rest in His control, His perfect timing, and plans for my future unknowns because my Lord's plans are far better than anything I could "ask or think" (Eph. 3:20). God's got this.

What do you re-discover about His sovereignty in these verses?

JOB 12:10

JOB 42:2

PSALM 135:5-7

PSALM 139:13-16

My prayer-song to You, sovereign Father

IN MY SUFFERING, YOU SAY THIS IS TRUE:

SO, IN MY SUFFERING, I PRAISE YOU BECAUSE:

IN MY SUFFERING, PLEASE HELP ME WITH:

INTO MY SUFFERING, I'LL SING THESE SONGS FROM MY PLAYLIST TO YOU TODAY:

God moves in a mysterious way
His wonders to perform.
He plants his footsteps in the sea
And rides upon the storm.

You fearful saints, fresh courage take;
The clouds you so much dread
Are big with mercy and shall break
In blessings on your head.

His purposes will ripen fast,
Unfolding ev'ry hour.
The bud may have a bitter taste,
But sweet will be the flow'r.

("GOD MOVES IN A MYSTERIOUS WAY," COWPER, W., 1774)

♪ ♪ ♪

Be still, my soul: the Lord is on your side;
bear patiently the cross of grief or pain;
leave to your God to order and provide;
in ev'ry change he faithful will remain.
Be still, my soul: your best, your heav'nly Friend
through thorny ways leads to a joyful end.

Be still, my soul: your God will undertake
to guide the future as he has the past.
Your hope, your confidence let nothing shake;
all now mysterious shall be bright at last.
Be still, my soul: the waves and winds still know
his voice who ruled them while he dwelt below.

("BE STILL, MY SOUL," VON SCHLEGEL, K.; TRANS. J. BOTHWICK, 1855)

DAY 4: KING OF KINGS AND LORD OF LORDS

$\mathcal{C}$risis threatened once again. Frightened, she prayed, "I'm so scared. Please help me." God reminded her in His Word, "The LORD has established his throne in the heavens, and his kingdom rules over all" (Ps. 103:19).

Her thoughts quieted, comforted by God's authoritative rule as "the blessed and only Sovereign, the King of kings and Lord of lords" (1 Tim. 6:15). Breathing into her anxiety about what might happen, she remembered He is:

"far above all rule and authority and power and dominion, and above every name that is named, not only in this age but also in the one to come" (Eph. 1:21).

He is the ruling King of kings. "He changes times and seasons; he removes kings and sets up kings" (Dan. 2:21). The Alpha and Omega (Rev. 1:8) is reigning right now, ruling over ALL, including the prowling enemy whose power is subject to His authority.

In wonder, she realized she was releasing her fear into the hands of her Savior and Lord, King Jesus. When the disciples saw him in resurrected glory, they worshiped Him, but some doubted. She heard His comfort to them, about her own situation, "All authority in heaven and on earth has been given to me" (Mt. 28:18). In her tearful surrender into peace, the King of kings calmed her: "And you have been filled in him, who is the head of *all* rule and authority" (Col. 2:10, emphasis added).

She walked into this crisis, freed from fear, knowing that her beloved Savior has full authority over the situation, as He accomplishes His redemptive kingdom work in and through it.

What do you re-discover about His Kingly authority in these verses?

2 CHRONICLES 20:6

PSALM 93:1-2

PSALM 74:12-13

REVELATION 17:14

My prayer-song to You, my King

IN MY SUFFERING, YOU SAY THIS IS TRUE:

SO, IN MY SUFFERING, I PRAISE YOU BECAUSE:

IN MY SUFFERING, PLEASE HELP ME WITH:

INTO MY SUFFERING, I'LL SING THESE SONGS FROM MY PLAYLIST TO YOU TODAY:

Rejoice, the Lord is King:
your Lord and King adore!
Rejoice, give thanks, and sing,
and triumph evermore.

Jesus the Savior reigns,
the God of truth and love;
when he had purged our stains,
he took his seat above.

His kingdom cannot fail,
he rules o'er earth and heav'n;
the keys of death and hell
are to our Jesus giv'n.

He sits at God's right hand
till all his foes submit,
and bow to his command,
and fall beneath his feet.

Rejoice in glorious hope!
Our Lord, the Judge, shall come,
and take his servants up
to their eternal home.

Lift up your heart, lift up your voice!
Rejoice, again I say, rejoice!

("REJOICE, THE LORD IS KING!," WESLEY, C., 1744)

♪ ♪ ♪

DAY 5: POWERFUL

*I*n these weak days, we cling to God's power. Theologians describe God's unlimited power as "omnipotent." He's able to do anything because He's all-powerful...over all things. We can rest because nothing can change His total power and that "He does all that He pleases" (Ps. 115:3). When Job cried to the Lord in his suffering, God vividly described His creative and sustaining power (Job 38-41). He is that powerful!

God says, "Have you commanded the morning since your days began, and caused the dawn to know its place" (Job 38:12)? "By the word of the LORD the heavens were made, and by the breath of his mouth all their host. He gathers the waters of the sea as a heap; he puts the deeps in storehouses. Let all the earth fear the LORD; let all the inhabitants of the world stand in awe of him! For he spoke, and it came to be; he commanded, and it stood firm" (Ps. 33:6-9).

Isn't it comforting that our heavenly Father drew us to Himself by this power (1 Cor. 1:18)? We are in Christ! On this side of the cross, Jesus "is the radiance of the glory of God and the exact imprint of his nature, and he upholds the universe *by the word of his power*" (Heb. 1:3, emphasis added).

In our weakness, as "sinners saved by grace" who suffer in this fallen world, He's also given "the immeasurable greatness of his power toward us who believe, according to the working of his great might that he worked in Christ when he raised him from the dead and seated him at his right hand in the heavenly places" (Eph. 1:19-20). Through His indwelling Spirit, He's strengthening us with His power (Eph. 3:16), as we suffer. We may feel weak, but our powerful Father is working to make us strong right now, helping us to trust His power (2 Cor. 12:10).

What do you re-discover about His power in these verses?

JEREMIAH 32:17

DEUTERONOMY 33:25

PSALM 147:5

EPHESIANS 3:20-21

My prayer-song to You, powerful Father

IN MY SUFFERING, YOU SAY THIS IS TRUE:

SO, IN MY SUFFERING, I PRAISE YOU BECAUSE:

IN MY SUFFERING, PLEASE HELP ME WITH:

INTO MY SUFFERING, I'LL SING THESE SONGS FROM MY PLAYLIST TO YOU TODAY:

I sing th'almighty pow'r of God
that made the mountains rise,
that spread the flowing seas abroad,
and built the lofty skies.
I sing the wisdom that ordained
the sun to rule the day;
the moon shines full at his command
and all the stars obey!

There's not a plant or flow'r below
but makes your glories known;
and clouds arise and tempests blow,
by order from your throne;
while all that borrows life from you
is ever in your care,
and everywhere that man can be,
you, God, are present there.

("I SING THE ALMIGHTY POWER OF GOD," WATTS, I., 1714)

♪ ♪ ♪

Supreme in wisdom as in pow'r
the Rock of Ages stands,
though him you cannot see, nor trace
the working of his hands.

("HAVE YOU NOT KNOWN, HAVE YOU NOT HEARD," WATTS, I., 1707)

DAY 6: KIND

*D*o you ever feel like your suffering negates God's kindness? Just as in the garden of Eden, is the lying enemy making you think the powerful and glorious King is more of a punishing tyrant with His children, rather than a kind King? Are you struggling to reconcile your suffering with God's kindness?

Let's battle the lies together. God says He's abundantly, plentifully kind. "Do you presume on the riches of his kindness…not knowing that God's kindness is meant to lead you to repentance?" (Rom. 2:4). There's a clue! God's kindness leads us to Jesus, in repentance. God's kindness shows us we need Jesus.

Remember the good news of the gospel? At the cross, Jesus took the entire punishment you and I deserve as sinners, born as "children of wrath" into this fallen world of sin (Eph. 2:3). There's no more punishment from God for us. His kindness led you to salvation, making you His child. Jesus' perfect righteousness, perfect kindness, was imputed or credited to you.

[He] "raised us up with him and seated us with him in the heavenly places in Christ Jesus, so that in the coming ages he might show the immeasurable riches of his grace in kindness toward us in Christ Jesus" (Eph. 2:6-7).

We have the "riches of His grace," receiving the kindness of God, now and forever. As in all of His attributes, God's kindness is unchanging and eternal.

Because Jesus is God, we see God's kindness in action, as we read about Him in the gospels. "Jesus is the same yesterday and today and forever" (Heb. 13:8). So, is it possible that, somehow, today's suffering is part of His kindness toward you, because you are in Christ?

Could it be that He's kindly pulling you near to Him in suffering? Kindly helping you see a deepened need for Him? Kindly leading you to repent? Let's run into His kindness toward us today.

What do you re-discover about His kindness in these verses?

HOSEA 11:4

TITUS 3:4-7

GALATIANS 5:22

My prayer-song to You, kind Father

IN MY SUFFERING, YOU SAY THIS IS TRUE:

SO, IN MY SUFFERING, I PRAISE YOU BECAUSE:

IN MY SUFFERING, PLEASE HELP ME WITH:

INTO MY SUFFERING, I'LL SING THESE SONGS FROM MY PLAYLIST TO YOU TODAY:

Let us, with a gladsome mind
praise the Lord, for he is kind:
for his mercies shall endure,
ever faithful, ever sure.

He has with a piteous eye
looked upon our misery:
for his mercies shall endure,
ever faithful, ever sure.

("LET US WITH A GLADSOME MIND," MILTON, J., 1623)

♪ ♪ ♪

Thy loving-kindness, Lord, is good and free:
in tender mercy turn thou unto me;
hide not thy face from me in my distress,
in mercy hear my pray'r, thy servant bless.

Needy and sorrowful, to thee I cry;
let thy salvation set my soul on high;
then I will sing and praise thy holy name;
my thankful song thy mercy shall proclaim.

With joy the meek shall see my soul restored;
your heart shall live, ye saints that seek the Lord;
he helps the needy and regards their cries,
those in distress the Lord will not despise.

Let heav'n above his grace and glory tell;
let earth and sea and all that in them dwell;
salvation to his people God will give,
and they that love his name with him shall live.

("THY LOVING-KINDNESS, LORD," HOPKINS, E. J., 1869)

DAY 7: GOOD

*I*n my suffering, I've had to beg God for His logical wisdom found in His Word. Since the Genesis 3 fall, our enemy hisses crafty lies that God is not good. Isn't good the opposite of evil? Satan, the embodiment of evil, wants to make us doubt God's goodness when we suffer. Let's battle the lies together today.

"You *are* good and *do* good; teach me your statutes" (Ps. 119:68, emphasis added). God plainly tells us that He is good. Over and over, He tells us to "give thanks to the Lord, *for He is good*" (e.g., Ps. 106, 107, 118, 136; 1 Chron. 16:34). Jesus tells us God alone is good (Mk. 10:18), Zechariah says His goodness is great (9:17), and Nahum reminds us the Lord is good, even in "the day of trouble" (1:7).

Ah, is that the hard thing? If God is always good and never evil, and He always *does* good because that's who He *is*, how does my trouble fit? In the Hebrew and Greek, the word "good" can mean pleasurable, but it also means something is valuable, with beneficial purpose. It's useful and upright. When God originally created all things, He called them "good." In His perfectly created Eden, all was good, pleasurable and useful. But, since the fall, we now live in a sin-infested world in which we desperately need to "hold fast to what is good" (Rom. 12:9) as we endure things that don't feel good.

"The LORD is good to those who wait for him, to the soul who seeks him. It is good that one should wait quietly for the salvation of the LORD" (Lam. 3:25-26).

Beloved, in the gospel of Jesus Christ, the *good* news for us, born as sinners into this sin-infested world, we've experienced God's goodness. Because God has led us to Jesus, He's given us what is good. As we wait for His restoration back to perfect goodness and elimination of sin and evil, we walk through trials, but as children of a loving Father (see Day 1). Consider the goodness of God as Jesus took our place on the cross. It was horrific as our Savior suffered our punishment on "Good" Friday. But it was valuable and necessary, far beyond any measure we would call good.

"Every good gift and every perfect gift is from above, coming down from the Father of lights, with whom there is no variation or shadow due to change" (Jas. 1:17).

Therefore, anything our Father allows us to suffer, though it is an evil thing, God means it for His good purposes (Gen. 50:20). "We know that for those who love God all things work together *for good*, for those who are called according to his purpose" (Rom. 8:28). God's goodness never changes, so this suffering must have a good purpose for us, in His good hands. Perhaps we can't see it yet. What are You teaching us, Lord?

"It is *good* for me that I was afflicted, that I might learn your statutes" (Ps. 119:71, emphasis added).

What do you re-discover about His goodness in these verses?

PSALM 52:8-9

MATTHEW 7:11

PSALM 23:6

PSALM 27:13

My prayer-song to You, good Father

IN MY SUFFERING, YOU SAY THIS IS TRUE:

SO, IN MY SUFFERING, I PRAISE YOU BECAUSE:

IN MY SUFFERING, PLEASE HELP ME WITH:

INTO MY SUFFERING, I'LL SING THESE SONGS FROM MY PLAYLIST TO YOU TODAY:

How good is the God we adore!
Our faithful, unchangeable friend:
his love is as great as his pow'r
and knows neither measure nor end.

For Christ is the first and the last;
his Spirit will guide us safe home;
we'll praise him for all that is past
and trust him for all that's to come.

(*"THIS GOD IS THE GOD WE ADORE," HART, J., 1857*)

♪ ♪ ♪
O praise the Lord, for he is good,
his mercies still endure;
thus say the ransomed of the Lord,
from all their foes secure.

(*"O PRAISE THE LORD, FOR HE IS GOOD," PUBLIC DOMAIN*)

DAY 8: ALL-KNOWING

The fancy word is "omniscient." God says He is all-knowing about the billions of simultaneous details...of everything. In my suffering, my thoughts easily wander into "what if." It's a comfort to know God is omniscient, far beyond what we could possibly know as mere humans. This is our God:

"Declaring the end from the beginning and from ancient times things not yet done, saying, 'My counsel shall stand, and I will accomplish all my purpose'" (Is. 46:10).

"Oh, the depth of the riches and wisdom and knowledge of God! How unsearchable are his judgments and how inscrutable his ways!" (Rom. 11:33)

He knows everything about us, numbering each of our hairs (Mt. 10:30), knowing the tiniest dysfunctional cell of our sick bodies, every situation and conversation, our every thought (Ps. 139:2-4; Eze. 11:5; 1 Chron. 28:9).

Does it scare you that He knows your every thought? My "what if" thoughts reveal my ongoing need for Jesus. "He knows our frame" (Ps. 103:14). Our thoughts alone reveal our sin. But, in His omniscient knowing, God knew we needed a Savior! He's executing His kingdom plan of all-knowing love for His children, prophesied and promised. Known.

"Jesus, delivered up according to the definite plan and foreknowledge of God, you crucified and killed by the hands of lawless men" (Acts 2:23).

And you, believer in Christ, are part of His kingdom plan. God knows we need His continual grace when we sin (Ps. 90:8; Rom. 5:8; 1 Jn. 3:20; Heb 4:13, 16). He knows our suffering creates a fresh dependence on His all-knowing and best way for us.

So, what can we do? Since He knows the future, knows us intimately as His children, and knows our deepest needs, we can pray for His guidance, wisdom, and strength to endure this suffering. Beloved in Christ, let's seek Him with this prayer: "Search me, O God, and know my heart! Try me and know my thoughts! And see if there be any grievous way in me, and lead me in the way everlasting!" (Ps. 139:23-24).

What do you re-discover about His omniscience in these verses?

JEREMIAH 1:5

PSALM 32:8

JOHN 10:14-15

COLOSSIANS 2:2-3

My prayer-song to You, all-knowing Father

In my suffering, You say this is true:

So, in my suffering, I praise You because:

In my suffering, please help me with:

Into my suffering, I'll sing these songs from my playlist to You today:

To God my earnest voice I raise,
to God my voice imploring prays;
before his face my grief I show
and tell my trouble and my woe.

When gloom and sorrow compass me,
the path I take is known to thee,
and all the toils that foes do lay
to snare thy servant in his way.

O Lord, my Savior, now to thee,
without a hope besides, I flee,
to thee, my shelter from the strife,
my portion in the land of life.

Be thou my help when troubles throng,
for I am weak and foes are strong;
my captive soul from prison bring,
and thankful praises I will sing.

("To God My Earnest Voice I Raise," Public domain)

♪ ♪ ♪

DAY 9: WISE

*O*ur all-knowing God is also perfectly wise, applying His wisdom within His love, kindness, goodness, power, and sovereign authority. He determines what's best and right because He created all things in His wisdom. Our wise God interweaves billions of simultaneous intricacies in His created universe.

"O LORD, how manifold are your works! In wisdom have you made them all; the earth is full of your creatures" (Ps. 104:24).

No one counsels, helps, or teaches the Lord (Prov. 21:30; Is. 40:13-14; Rom. 11:34). In the last chapters of Job, God answers Job's suffering heart-cries by describing His glorious, stand-alone wisdom in all things. Because God's wisdom includes His goodness and love, we know He never makes a mistake. We can rest in His wisdom.

Beloved, we don't understand, do we? How could we? We are not God and we have limited wisdom.

"For my thoughts are not your thoughts, neither are your ways my ways, declares the LORD. For as the heavens are higher than the earth, so are my ways higher than your ways and my thoughts than your thoughts" (Is. 55:8-9).

So, when our limited understanding brings emotional distress in suffering, how can we respond to our wise God?

"The fear of the LORD is the beginning of wisdom, and the knowledge of the Holy One is insight" (Prov. 9:10). Worship of God, as He's revealed Himself to be in the Bible, is our wise response as we suffer. Our suffering hearts turn to reverent awe, respect, and honor. We turn to our Savior Jesus Christ who is "the power...and wisdom of God" (1 Cor. 1:24). We seek His wisdom on how to deal Biblically with our suffering (Jas. 3:17). Let's discover God's wisdom for us in this season of suffering, beloved in Christ.

What do you re-discover about His wisdom and our response in these verses?

DANIEL 2:20-22

JAMES 1:5-6

ROMANS 16:25-27

My prayer-song to You, wise Father

IN MY SUFFERING, YOU SAY THIS IS TRUE:

SO, IN MY SUFFERING, I PRAISE YOU BECAUSE:

IN MY SUFFERING, PLEASE HELP ME WITH:

INTO MY SUFFERING, I'LL SING THESE SONGS FROM MY PLAYLIST TO YOU TODAY:

Immortal, invisible, God only wise,
in light inaccessible hid from our eyes,
most blessed, most glorious, the Ancient of Days,
almighty, victorious, thy great name we praise.

Unresting, unhasting and silent as light,
nor wanting, nor wasting, thou rulest in might;
thy justice like mountains high soaring above
thy clouds which are fountains of goodness and love.

Great Father of glory, pure Father of light,
thine angels adore thee, all veiling their sight;
all praise we would render; O help us to see
'tis only the splendor of light hideth thee!

("IMMORTAL, INVISIBLE, GOD ONLY WISE," SMITH, W.C., *1867*)

♪ ♪ ♪
To God the only wise,
our Savior and our King,
let all the saints below the skies
their humble praises bring.

To our Redeemer God
wisdom and pow'r belongs,
immortal crowns of majesty,
and everlasting songs.

("TO GOD THE ONLY WISE," WATTS, I., PUBLIC DOMAIN)

DAY 10: PRESENT EVERYWHERE

*G*od is omnipresent. He's everywhere, always there, outside of what we consider as time or place. He is "the Alpha and Omega, the first and the last, the beginning and the end" (Rev. 22:13), infinite in all ways. When we consider His all-knowing, always wise, sovereign goodness and love, it's so comforting to know that He is also always present.

God guided the Israelites with His presence. As they wandered to the promised land, He "went before them by day in a pillar of cloud" and "by night in a pillar of fire to give them light, that they might travel by day and by night" (Ex. 13:21). His presence never left them, even in the worst of their suffering.

Since the fall in Genesis 3, evil and suffering are part of this earthly life. Our inborn sin makes us want to hide from God's presence (Gen. 3:8). Our sin makes us doubt the One whose "eyes...are in every place, keeping watch on the evil and the good" (Prov. 15:3), who looks from His heavenly throne on each of us, always (Ps. 33:13-14).

"Am I a God at hand, declares the LORD, and not a God far away? Can a man hide himself in secret places so that I cannot see him? declares the LORD. Do I not fill heaven and earth? declares the LORD" (Jer. 23:23-24).

Could praising God be a path toward trusting God, precisely because He's present in all places and events of past, present, and future? Even in today's suffering?

Solomon praised God's presence, in wonder. "Behold, heaven and the highest heaven cannot contain you" (1 Kgs. 8:27). The Lord exhorts us, "Come into his presence with singing!" (Ps. 110:2), "Let us come into his presence with thanksgiving" (Ps. 95:2). Today, let's praise our always-present God, as we suffer, because He is always present, everywhere.

What do you re-discover about His presence in these verses?

DEUTERONOMY 31:6

ISAIAH 43:2

PSALM 139:7-10

My prayer-song to You, always present Father

IN MY SUFFERING, YOU SAY THIS IS TRUE:

SO, IN MY SUFFERING, I PRAISE YOU BECAUSE:

IN MY SUFFERING, PLEASE HELP ME WITH:

INTO MY SUFFERING, I'LL SING THESE SONGS FROM MY PLAYLIST TO YOU TODAY:

God dwells in Heaven: He rules above,
In everlasting might,
Beyond where stars their courses move,
In uncreated light.

God dwells on earth; and all around
We view His wondrous power;
His terrors in the thunder sound,
His mercies in the shower.

When man erects a house of prayer,
There God resides within,
To witness every feeling there,
And pardon every sin.

O, let me find Thee everywhere—
Around me, and within!
Be every day a day of prayer,
And pure from every sin.

("THE DWELLING PLACE OF GOD," WARE, H., 1813)

♪ ♪ ♪

There's not a plant or flow'r below
but makes your glories known;
and clouds arise and tempests blow,
by order from your throne;
while all that borrows life from you
is ever in your care,
and everywhere that man can be,
you, God, are present there.

("I SING THE ALMIGHTY POWER OF GOD," WATTS, I., PUBLIC DOMAIN)

DAY 11: PRESENT WITH ME

*I*f God is always present, then He is always present with you. He is always with you in your suffering. He is always accessible. The word presence literally means "face" so He is facing you, seeing you, knowing you, with you. Beloved in Christ, remember that Jesus is Immanuel, "God with us" (Is. 7:14; Mt. 1:22-23).

"The Word became flesh and dwelt among us, and we have seen his glory, glory as of the only Son from the Father, full of grace and truth" (Jn. 1:14). The glorious One who made all things, who's present everywhere and in all of time as we know it, is with you personally.

By God's grace, "even when we were dead in our trespasses, [He] made us alive together with Christ...and raised us up with him and seated us with him in the heavenly places" (Eph. 2:5-6). The Lord made us alive and now we are *with Christ.* You may not feel like it when suffering screams loud, but He woke us up this morning and we are alive by Him, through Him, and for Him, by His gift and with His abundant love and grace for today's challenge.

Because we are *in Christ,* the Holy Spirit now dwells within us (1 Cor. 3:16). As we suffer, He's our strength, our guide, our comforter, our helper, always-present. He is "the guarantee of our inheritance until we acquire possession of it, to the praise of his glory" (Eph. 1:14).

And that inheritance? This is our hope! We will dwell face to face with Him forever in His personal presence that we can actually see!

"And I heard a loud voice from the throne saying, 'Behold, the dwelling place of God is with man. He will dwell with them, and they will be his people, and God himself will be with them as their God.'" (Rev. 21:3).

Beloved, as we wait for that glorious day, we have constant access to Him in prayer, possessing God's continual presence with us as we suffer in this fallen world.

What do you re-discover about His presence with you in these verses?

PSALM 16:11

MATTHEW 28:20

ROMANS 8:26-27

My prayer-song to You, God who is always present with me:

IN MY SUFFERING, YOU SAY THIS IS TRUE:

SO, IN MY SUFFERING, I PRAISE YOU BECAUSE:

IN MY SUFFERING, PLEASE HELP ME WITH:

INTO MY SUFFERING, I'LL SING THESE SONGS FROM MY PLAYLIST TO YOU TODAY:

Love divine, all loves excelling,
Joy of heav'n, to earth come down:
fix in us thy humble dwelling,
all thy faithful mercies crown:
Jesus, thou art all compassion,
pure, unbounded love thou art;
visit us with thy salvation,
enter ev'ry trembling heart.

Breathe, O breathe thy loving Spirit
into ev'ry troubled breast;
let us all in thee inherit,
let us find the promised rest:
take away the love of sinning;
Alpha and Omega be;
End of faith, as its Beginning,
set our hearts at liberty.

Finish, then, thy new creation;
pure and spotless let us be:
let us see thy great salvation
perfectly restored in thee;
changed from glory into glory,
till in heav'n we take our place,
till we cast our crowns before thee,
lost in wonder, love, and praise.

("LOVE DIVINE, ALL LOVES EXCELLING," WESLEY, C., 1747)

♪ ♪ ♪

Rejoice! Rejoice! Immanuel
shall come to you, O Israel.

("O COME, O COME, IMMANUEL," 12TH C., TRANS. NEALE, J. M., 1851)

DAY 12: UNCHANGING

God tells us that His throne "is forever and ever, He is "the same," and His "years will have no end" (Heb. 1:8a, 12b). The Lord is immutable, through all of history and in all of His attributes. "For I the LORD do not change" (Mal. 3:6). Psalm 100:5 refers to His character (goodness, steadfast love, faithfulness) as one that "endures forever...to all generations." All? That means you and me. Today.

Let's consider yesterday. Remembering that Jesus is the image of God, God Himself (Col. 1:15), we see the character of God in the words and actions of Jesus. It's amazing to study the gospels and experience the Lord there. But if our Lord is the same always, the God of the Old Testament is the same as the God of the New. The entire Bible is one glorious kingdom story of our unchanging God creating perfection, redeeming fallen people whose sin destroyed perfection, and one day restoring all things to perfection. In all His actions, His ways are unchanging because He is unchanging.

"Lift up your eyes to the heavens, and look at the earth beneath; for the heavens vanish like smoke, the earth will wear out like a garment, and they who dwell in it will die in like manner, but my salvation will be forever, and my righteousness will never be dismayed" (Is. 51:6).

If our unchanging God has become our intimate Father through Christ, continually at work in our lives to make us more and more like Jesus (1 Thess. 5:23), His *unchanging* attributes become anchors for our soul as we suffer. From the beginning to end of all time and history as we know it, "the counsel of the LORD stands forever, the plans of his heart to all generations" (Ps. 33:11). James comforts us not to believe the lies that God changes as we suffer: "There is no variation or shadow due to change" with our "Father of lights" (1:17). So, our God is the same…in the suffering we are enduring today. Let's go back to Hebrews 1 for a moment. Do you see? This is our beloved Savior, Jesus!

So tomorrow? We can rest and hope in God's eternal promises for tomorrow, resting in His unchanging character. We can trust that His plan for His children won't change, yesterday, today, and forever.

"But he is unchangeable, and who can turn him back? What he desires, that he does. For he *will* complete what he appoints for me, and many such things are in his mind" (Job 23:13-14, emphasis added).

What do you re-discover about His unchanging essence in these verses?

Psalm 102:25-28

Numbers 23:19

Hebrews 13:8

My prayer-song to You, unchanging God

IN MY SUFFERING, YOU SAY THIS IS TRUE:

SO, IN MY SUFFERING, I PRAISE YOU BECAUSE:

IN MY SUFFERING, PLEASE HELP ME WITH:

INTO MY SUFFERING, I'LL SING THESE SONGS FROM MY PLAYLIST TO YOU TODAY:

Great is thy faithfulness, O God my Father;
there is no shadow of turning with thee;
thou changest not, thy compassions, they fail not;
as thou hast been thou forever wilt be.

Summer and winter and springtime and harvest.
sun, moon, and stars in their courses above.
join with all nature in manifold witness
to thy great faithfulness, mercy, and love.

("GREAT IS THY FAITHFULNESS," CHISHOLM, T. O., 1923)

♪ ♪ ♪

Great God, how infinite art thou!
How poor and weak are we!
Let the whole race of creatures bow,
And pay their praise to thee.

Eternity, with all its years,
Stands present in thy view;
To thee there's nothing old appears;
To thee there's nothing new.

("GREAT GOD! HOW INFINITE ART THOU!", WATTS, I., PUBLIC DOMAIN)

DAY 13: TRUSTWORTHY

"The LORD is my rock and my fortress and my deliverer, my God, my rock, in whom I take refuge, my shield, and the horn of my salvation, my stronghold" (Ps. 18:2). Our Father calls Himself a rock! Think about rocks—they're strong, secure, solid, safe, immovable in the harshest of wind, rain, or drought. When we need sturdy and solid, we build with rock.

When God described Jesus in the Old Testament prophecies, one metaphor He used was Jesus as "cornerstone" (Is. 28:16; Ps. 118:22). The cornerstone holds up the building, a solid rock that's firm, perfectly aligning the entire structure. It's trustworthy. The Lord is trustworthy; the "tested...costly...firmly placed" cornerstone of Jesus (Is. 28:16) holds our secure salvation because it all "came about from the Lord" (Mt. 21:42).

It's so easy for me to forget God's trustworthy hold on me as I suffer. It's so easy to forget my trustworthy Rock of ages as I focus on the pain I'm enduring. My troubles scream loud and I quickly fixate on them, spiral into desperate fix-it mode, or helpless despair. "For you have forgotten the God of your salvation and have not remembered the Rock of your refuge" (Is. 17:10-11).

Let's remember. Let's ask for His forgiveness. Let's run back to our trustworthy Rock, seeking and drinking deeply from His Word as the Spirit helps us hear and trust the voice of Jesus yet again.

"For they drank from the spiritual Rock that followed them, and the Rock was Christ" (1 Cor. 10:4).

"But whoever drinks of the water that I will give him will never be thirsty again. The water that I will give him will become in him a spring of water welling up to eternal life" (Jn. 4:14).

What do you re-discover about His trustworthiness in these verses?

PSALM 119:89, 152

ISAIAH 40:8

MATTHEW 5:18

PSALM 95:1

My prayer-song to You, trustworthy Father

IN MY SUFFERING, YOU SAY THIS IS TRUE:

SO, IN MY SUFFERING, I PRAISE YOU BECAUSE:

IN MY SUFFERING, PLEASE HELP ME WITH:

INTO MY SUFFERING, I'LL SING THESE SONGS FROM MY PLAYLIST TO YOU TODAY:

Rock of Ages, cleft for me
let me hide myself in thee;
let the water and the blood,
from thy riven side which flowed,
be of sin the double cure,
cleanse me from its guilt and pow'r.

Nothing in my hand I bring,
simply to thy cross I cling;
naked, come to thee for dress;
helpless, look to thee for grace;
foul, I to the Fountain fly;
wash me, Savior, or I die.

Not the labors of my hands
can fulfil thy law's demands;
could my zeal no respite know,
could my tears for ever flow,
all for sin could not atone;
thou must save, and thou alone.

While I draw this fleeting breath,
when mine eyelids close in death,
when I soar to worlds unknown,
see thee on thy judgment throne,
Rock of Ages, cleft for me,
let me hide myself in thee.

("ROCK OF AGES, CLEFT FOR ME," TOPLADY, A., 1776)

♪ ♪ ♪

DAY 14: FAITHFUL AND TRUE

*T*he book of Lamentations is a book of agony. Everything was falling apart as God's people suffered from their unfaithful sin and its horrific effects. In the middle of the writer's grief, he tells his soul an important truth about God: "Great is your faithfulness" (Lam. 3:23).

God is faithful. Greatly faithful. Although many think that means He will give us what we want, the Hebrew word literally means that He is firm, steadfast, steady, and gives us His fidelity (like a perfect marriage vow). Unlike human beings, His faithfulness is always sure, because He can't be unfaithful to His children. It's who He is.

He never lies (Numb. 23:19) and His Word (Scripture) is truth (Jn. 17:17). Beloved in Christ, what is the most-true evidence of His faithfulness to you? It's Jesus Himself, the One who says He is "the way, and the *truth*, and the life. No one comes to the Father except through me" (Jn. 14:6). So, what's promised to those who are His? In Jesus, the Lord's faithful, firm, covenant love has been fulfilled.

"Know therefore that the LORD your God is God, the faithful God who keeps covenant and steadfast love with those who love him and keep his commandments, to a thousand generations" (Deut. 7:9).

What does this mean in our suffering today? Believers can hear

His voice in Scripture and know it's true, firm, sure. God helps us trust Himself...today.

"But the Lord is faithful. He will establish you and guard you against the evil one" (2 Thess. 3:3).

God helps us trust Him with tomorrow. We can trust that the Word made flesh, Jesus Christ our Lord (Jn. 1) is Faithful and True (Rev. 19:11). Beloved, our suffering will come to an end one day. We have complete hope for tomorrow, because He is going to return, restore all things, and make all things new. It's a true promise.

"Then I saw heaven opened, and behold, a white horse! The one sitting on it is called Faithful and True, and in righteousness he judges and makes war" (Rev. 19:11).

Let's keep going, beloved! Let's keep believing His faithfulness to us! Let's fight the lies of the enemy with His truth, with Scripture.

What do you re-discover about His true faithfulness in these verses?

2 Timothy 2:13

John 8:31-32

1 John 1:9

Psalm 89:1-8

My prayer-song to You, faithful and true Lord:

IN MY SUFFERING, YOU SAY THIS IS TRUE:

SO, IN MY SUFFERING, I PRAISE YOU BECAUSE:

IN MY SUFFERING, PLEASE HELP ME WITH:

INTO MY SUFFERING, I'LL SING THESE SONGS FROM MY PLAYLIST TO YOU TODAY:

Great is Thy faithfulness!
Great is Thy faithfulness!
Morning by morning, new mercies I see:
All I have needed thy hand hath provided—
Great is Thy faithfulness, Lord, unto me.

Pardon for sin and a peace that endureth,
Thine own dear presence to cheer and to guide;
Strength for today and bright hope for tomorrow,
Blessings all mine, with ten thousand beside.

("GREAT IS THY FAITHFULNESS," CHISHOLM, T. O., 1923)

♪ ♪ ♪

Have you not known, have you not heard
That firm remains on high
The everlasting throne of him
who formed the earth and sky?

Are you afraid his pow'r shall fail
when comes your evil day?
And can an all-creating arm
Grow weary or decay?

Supreme in wisdom as in pow'r
The Rock of Ages stands.
Though him you cannot see,
Nor trace the working of his hands.

He gives the conquest to the weak,
Supports the fainting heart;
And courage in the evil hour
His heavenly aids impart.

("HAVE YOU NOT KNOWN, HAVE YOU NOT HEARD," WATTS, I., 1707)

DAY 15: JUST AND FAIR

od says He is just and fair. His actions and works are then also just and fair (Deut. 32:4). Sometimes we cringe, "What if this suffering is His judgment on me?"

Beloved in Christ, our just God must punish our inborn sin with His wrath (Rom. 1:18). He wouldn't be just or fair if He didn't, because "all have sinned and fall short of the glory of God" (Rom. 3:23) and "God is a righteous judge" (Ps. 7:11). But this is why He gave us Jesus! Jesus took all of the sin of believing Christians and experienced our Father's just and fair wrath against sin and just punishment. All of it. On the cross, He cried, "My God, my God, why have you forsaken me?" (Ps. 22:1) as God's justice was served. He paid the full debt owed to God for your sin and mine. What wondrous love is this.

"Therefore, since we have been justified by faith, we have peace with God through our Lord Jesus Christ" (Rom. 5:1). "There is therefore now *no condemnation* for those who are in Christ Jesus" (Rom. 8:1, emphasis mine).

Your suffering is not condemnation. Like any loving parent or teacher provides, it may be discipline to help you learn something and correct you (Heb. 12:7-11). But His just wrath has been satisfied for you, by Christ. One of my favorite pastors reminds believers, "God is not mad at you."

As global suffering worsens, we read of Christ's return to judge all sin and we cringe for those who aren't His. Because God is just and fair, His wrath and punishment for sin is indeed coming. Time will be up on that day and unbelievers will cry to the mountains and rocks, "Fall on us and hide us from the face of him who is seated on the throne, and from the wrath of the Lamb" (Rev. 6:16).

Could your suffering be a new time of urgency for you to share the gospel with others? Could you help others see that our just God gave Jesus, perfectly obedient and righteous? His death and resurrection satisfied all of God's just requirements! Is it time to share your gospel hope? Who might you pray for, as you walk through your pain? How could each day of your current suffering include rejoicing in the person and work of Christ, the good news of the gospel? Knowing God's justice has been satisfied for your sin, by Jesus, what is He teaching you through this suffering? Run to His Word and He will instruct You!

What do you re-discover about His justice and fairness in these verses?

PSALM 75:1-7

2 THESSALONIANS 1:5-10

ISAIAH 30:18

My prayer-song to You, just and fair Lord:

In my suffering, You say this is true:

So, in my suffering, I praise You because

In my suffering, please help me with:

Into my suffering, I'll sing these songs from my playlist to You today:

Day of judgment! Day of wonders!
Hark! the trumpet's awful sound,
louder than a thousand thunders,
shakes the vast creation round.

Careless sinner,
what will then become of thee?
But to those who have confessed,
loved and served the Lord below,
he will say, "Come near, ye blessed,
see the kingdom I bestow;
you forever shall my love and glory know."

("DAY OF JUDGMENT! DAY OF WONDERS!," NEWTON, J., 1774)

♪ ♪ ♪

Jesus paid it all,
all to him I owe;
sin had left a crimson stain,
he washed it white as snow.

For nothing good have I
whereby your grace to claim —
I'll wash my garments white
in the blood of Calv'ry's lamb.

I hear the Savior say,
"Your strength indeed is small,
child of weakness, watch and pray,
find in me your all in all."

("JESUS PAID IT ALL," HALL, E. M., 1865)

DAY 16: HOLY, PERFECT, SET APART, PURE

*O*ur unchanging and just God is holy, holy, holy. He is set apart in essence, separate from evil, from sin. In His perfection and purity, He is unique, unlike us and unlike gods of all other religions.

"Who is like you, O LORD, among the gods? Who is like you, majestic in holiness, awesome in glorious deeds, doing wonders?" (Ex. 15:11)

Through Scripture's glimpses of His throne in heaven, we hear unending song lyrics. Worship is the natural response to God's holiness, in awe and reverence. He's calling us to also worship and honor Him as holy.

"Holy, holy, holy is the LORD of hosts; the whole earth is full of his glory!" (Is. 6:3)

"Holy, holy, holy, is the Lord God Almighty, who was and is and is to come!" (Rev. 4:8)

"Who will not fear, O Lord, and glorify your name? For you alone are holy. All nations will come and worship you, for your righteous acts have been revealed" (Rev. 15:4).

The Holy One asks us, "To whom then will you compare me, that I should be like him?" (Is. 40:25)

In our suffering, this thrice holy God is calling us to something new, setting us apart as His redeemed children in Christ. He's calling us to "be renewed in the spirit of your minds, and to put on the new self, created after the likeness of God in true righteousness and holiness" (Eph. 4:23-24).

In this sanctifying time of suffering, He's making us more holy, more like Jesus, until we enter His holy presence for eternity, "in order to present you holy and blameless and above reproach before him" (Col. 1:22). How could this time be one of "spiritual worship" as He transforms you "by the renewal of your mind" (Rom. 12:1-2)? To begin, let's worship and praise God as holy, holy, holy.

What do you re-discover about His perfect holiness in these verses?

PSALM 99:1-3

PSALM 96:9

2 CORINTHIANS 7:1

1 THESSALONIANS 3:12-13

My prayer-song to you, holy, holy, holy Lord:

IN MY SUFFERING, YOU SAY THIS IS TRUE:

SO, IN MY SUFFERING, I PRAISE YOU BECAUSE:

IN MY SUFFERING, PLEASE HELP ME WITH:

INTO MY SUFFERING, I'LL SING THESE SONGS FROM MY PLAYLIST TO YOU TODAY:

Holy, holy, holy! Lord God Almighty!
Early in the morning our song shall rise to thee.
Holy, holy, holy! Merciful and mighty!
God in three Persons, blessed Trinity!

Holy, holy, holy! All the saints adore thee,
casting down their golden crowns
around the glassy sea;
cherubim and seraphim falling down before thee,
who wert, and art, and evermore shalt be.

Holy, holy, holy! Though the darkness hide thee,
though the eye of sinful man thy glory may not see,
only thou art holy; there is none beside thee
perfect in pow'r, in love, and purity.

Holy, holy, holy! Lord God Almighty!
All thy works shall praise thy name in earth and sky and sea.
Holy, holy, holy! Merciful and mighty!
God in three Persons, blessed Trinity!

("HOLY, HOLY, HOLY," HEBER, R., 1826)

♪ ♪ ♪

Thy mighty name salvation is,
and keeps my happy soul above;
comfort it brings, and pow'r and peace,
and joy and everlasting love:
to me, with thy dear name, are giv'n
pardon and holiness and heav'n.

("THOU HIDDEN SOURCE OF CALM REPOSE," WESLEY, C., 1749)

DAY 17: GRACIOUS

*G*od says, "As he who called you is holy, you also be holy in all your conduct...You shall be holy, for I am holy" (1 Pet. 1:15-16). In suffering? Acting like Jesus in *all* our conduct? It seems impossible, doesn't it? We need His grace, every moment. Hallelujah, God is gracious!

"The LORD is gracious and merciful, slow to anger and abounding in steadfast love" (Ps. 145:8).

Because He is gracious, He gives us unmerited, undeserved favor or grace. We are His children because of His saving grace. It's His gift because there's nothing we did or can do to earn it (Rom. 3:24; 5:15, 20). He lavished the riches of His grace upon His adopted children: "redemption through his blood, the forgiveness of our trespasses" (Eph. 1:7).

So, how does this apply to a suffering believer? Does our suffering mean our faith isn't strong enough for His grace or favor? That His saving grace seemed to be in the past and it's gone now that we're suffering?

"For by grace you have been saved through faith. And this is not your own doing; it is the gift of God, not a result of works, so that no one may boast" (Eph. 2:8-9).

Who gave us initial faith, according to Eph. 2? Who is now perfecting our faith, in this time of suffering, beloved? Our faith is a gift of His grace…past, present, and future.

"Jesus, the *founder and perfecter* of our faith, who for the joy that was set before him endured the cross, despising the shame, and is seated at the right hand of the throne of God" (Heb. 12:2, emphasis mine).

Because our God is always gracious, each of us are sinners saved by grace (Eph. 4:7). By His gift, He's reconciled us to Himself in order to present us "holy and blameless" (Col. 1:22). By His grace, He's strengthening us as we suffer (2 Tim. 2:1). With His favor, we have hope for our future. "And after you have suffered a little while, the God of all grace, who has called you to his eternal glory in Christ, will himself restore, confirm, strengthen, and establish you" (1 Pet. 5:10).

As we wait for His final restoration of all things, walking through suffering in this fallen world, our gracious God perfects and strengthens us daily, giving us the hope and faith we need. It's all His gift to us. Let's receive it today.

What do you re-discover about His grace in these verses?

2 Corinthians 12:9

Romans 6:14

Titus 2:11-14

My prayer-song to You, gracious Lord:

IN MY SUFFERING, YOU SAY THIS IS TRUE:

SO, IN MY SUFFERING, I PRAISE YOU BECAUSE:

IN MY SUFFERING, PLEASE HELP ME WITH:

INTO MY SUFFERING, I'LL SING THESE SONGS FROM MY PLAYLIST TO YOU TODAY:

Amazing grace!– how sweet the sound–
that saved a wretch like me!
I once was lost, but now am found,
was blind, but now I see.

'Twas grace that taught my heart to fear,
and grace my fears relieved;
how precious did that grace appear
the hour I first believed!

Thro' many dangers, toils and snares,
I have already come;
'tis grace has brought me safe thus far,
and grace will lead me home.

The Lord has promised good to me,
his Word my hope secures;
he will my shield and portion be,
as long as life endures.

And when this flesh and heart shall fail,
and mortal life shall cease,
I shall possess within the veil
a life of joy and peace.

When we've been there ten thousand years,
bright shining as the sun,
we've no less days to sing God's praise
than when we've first begun.

("AMAZING GRACE," NEWTON, J., 1779)

♪ ♪ ♪

DAY 18: RIGHTEOUS

od says He is perfectly righteous, so all He does is always right (Ps. 145:17; Is. 45:21; Zeph. 3:5). His righteousness reaches to the high heavens (Ps. 71:19)! There is zero unrighteousness in Him.

How could God be righteous when suffering is happening to me? When these questions float through my mind, I need to remember the gospel, "the power of God for salvation to everyone who believes...For in it the righteousness of God is revealed from faith *for faith*, as it is written, 'The righteous shall live by faith'" (Rom. 1:16-17, emphasis added).

Remembering that no human is righteous (Rom. 3:10) and that the righteousness of God has been demonstrated to all who believe, through faith in Jesus Christ (Rom. 3:21-22), we realize this suffering is a time to live by that same faith. Suffering may not feel "right" to us, yet God is not only righteous, but He's graciously made us "a new creation...in Christ" (2 Cor. 5:17). He has "not counted our trespasses against" us (2 Cor. 5:19), but now, when our Father sees us, He sees the righteousness of Christ.

"For our sake he made him to be sin who knew no sin, so that in him we might become the righteousness of God" (2 Cor. 5:21). "And because of [God] you are in Christ Jesus, who became to us wisdom from God, righteousness and sanctification and redemption" (1 Cor. 1:30).

In this amazing exchange of our sin and the perfect righteousness of Jesus, this means the Lord is continually at work to sanctify us, set us apart, and make us more and more like our precious Savior.

Somehow, this suffering today, in His righteous hands, is a mysterious part of His righteous work in our lives.

"For Christ also suffered once for sins, the righteous for the unrighteous, that he might bring us to God, being put to death in the flesh but made alive in the spirit" (1 Pet. 3:18).

One day, after fighting the good fight and keeping the faith, by His daily grace, we will receive "the crown of righteousness...laid up for me...which the Lord the righteous judge will award" to each of us "who have loved his appearing" on the day we see Him face to face (2 Tim. 4:7-8). Let's look forward, with hope, and remind ourselves that what is happening is in the hand of our righteous God.

What do you re-discover about His righteousness and our response, in these verses?

MATTHEW 5:6

MATTHEW 6:33

REVELATION 15:3-4

My prayer-song to You, righteous Lord:

IN MY SUFFERING, YOU SAY THIS IS TRUE:

SO, IN MY SUFFERING, I PRAISE YOU BECAUSE:

IN MY SUFFERING, PLEASE HELP ME WITH:

INTO MY SUFFERING, I'LL SING THESE SONGS FROM MY PLAYLIST TO YOU TODAY:

My hope is built on nothing less
than Jesus' blood and righteousness;
I dare not trust the sweetest frame,
but wholly lean on Jesus' name.

When darkness veils his lovely face,
I rest on his unchanging grace;
in every high and stormy gale
my anchor holds within the veil.

On Christ, the solid rock, I stand;
all other ground is sinking sand.

("MY HOPE IS BUILT ON NOTHING LESS," MOTE, E., 1834)

♪ ♪ ♪

Here, O my Lord, I see thee face to face;
here would I touch and handle things unseen,
here grasp with firmer hand th'eternal grace,
and all my weariness upon thee lean.

Mine is the sin, but thine the righteousness;
mine is the guilt, but thine the cleansing blood;
here is my robe, my refuge, and my peace:
thy blood, thy righteousness, O Lord my God.

("HERE, O MY LORD, I SEE THEE FACE TO FACE," BONAR, H., 1855)

DAY 19: REFUGE

"God is our refuge and strength, a very present help in trouble. Therefore we will not fear though the earth gives way, though the mountains be moved into the heart of the sea, though its waters roar and foam, though the mountains tremble at its swelling. Selah" (Ps. 46:1-3).

God's character and attributes mean He is *the* refuge for His suffering children. Because of who He is, unchanging in all His attributes, we are safe and secure in His protection. He shelters us, not always *from* troubles in this fallen world of sin, but cocoons us as we go *through* them. He is our refuge of strength, help, and eternal hope on our suffering days (Jer. 16:19).

Why? How? Remember that "God so loved the world, that he gave his only Son, that whoever believes in him should not perish but have eternal life" (Jn. 3:16). When He tells us to "take the helmet of salvation" as a battle tool (Eph. 6:17) or the "hope of salvation...for a helmet" (1 Thess. 5:8), He's telling us to take refuge in our sure salvation when suffering attacks our thoughts.

Over and over, daily and constantly, we run to our refuge as those in Christ. We abide in Jesus (Jn. 15:4), dwelling there, remaining there. We rehearse the gospel to our thoughts, pray-singing of His safe and secure and saving strength. We hear, read, study His Word. We pray for His help at every moment. We trust what He says, because "he who dwells in the shelter of the Most High *will* abide in the shadow of the Almighty" (Ps. 91:1, emphasis added) and "He who began a good work in you *will* bring it to completion at the day of Jesus Christ" (Phil. 1:6, emphasis added).

Let's rest in God's beautiful promise. As we rest, abide, re-turn to the Lord and the saving and transforming work of His Spirit in our lives, He helps us trust Him as our refuge in the midst of our suffering.

What do you re-discover about God as your refuge in these verses?

PSALM 91:1-2

PSALM 62:7-8

HEBREWS 6:18

My prayer-song to You, my Refuge:

IN MY SUFFERING, YOU SAY THIS IS TRUE:

SO, IN MY SUFFERING, I PRAISE YOU BECAUSE:

IN MY SUFFERING, PLEASE HELP ME WITH:

INTO MY SUFFERING, I'LL SING THESE SONGS FROM MY PLAYLIST TO YOU TODAY:

How firm a foundation, you saints of the Lord,
is laid for your faith in his excellent Word!
What more can he say than to you he has said,
to you who for refuge to Jesus have fled?

"Fear not, I am with you, O be not dismayed;
for I am your God, and will still give you aid;
I'll strengthen you, help you, and cause you to stand,
upheld by my righteous, omnipotent hand.

When through the deep waters I call you to go,
the rivers of sorrow shall not overflow;
for I will be with you, your troubles to bless,
and sanctify to you your deepest distress.

When through fiery trials your pathway shall lie,
my grace, all-sufficient, shall be your supply;
the flame shall not hurt you; I only design
your dross to consume and your gold to refine.

E'en down to old age all my people shall prove
my sovereign, eternal, unchangeable love;
and when hoary hairs shall their temples adorn,
like lambs they shall still in my bosom be borne.

The soul that on Jesus has leaned for repose,
I will not, I will not desert to his foes;
that soul, though all hell should endeavor to shake,
I'll never, no never, no never forsake."

("How Firm a Foundation," K., 1787)

♪ ♪ ♪

DAY 20: STRONG

Our powerful God created, sustains, and judges the entire world. We see His power every morning and evening, with the rising of the sun, moon, and stars. We see it in the tiniest of His created creatures, the wonder of our intricately made bodies, the magnificence of ecosystems.

God's Word tells us He is also strong and mighty. "Who is this King of glory? The LORD, strong and mighty, the LORD, mighty in battle!" (Ps. 24:8). Because He is supremely strong, He can do anything. His work as creator proves this (Jer. 32:17) and His role as "the LORD, God of all flesh" proves this (Jer. 32:27). He repeats this question often, "Is anything too hard" for God? (e.g., Gen. 18:14; Jer. 32:27) and answers, "For nothing will be impossible with God" (Lk. 1:37).

Beloved, Luke 1 announces the birth of our Savior. In God's surpassing strength, by the Holy Spirit, He brought Jesus into the world, overriding His natural creation. And who is our Savior? "Wonderful Counselor, *Mighty God*, Everlasting Father, Prince of Peace" (Is. 9:6, emphasis added). Prophesied 700 years prior to His birth, Jesus is Mighty God.

The prophet Zephaniah offered joy amidst crisis as he encouraged

God's people not to fear evil or weaken as our final day of this fallen world approaches. He reminded them who is with them: "a mighty one who will save" (Zeph. 3:17). And indeed, the Lord has fulfilled this prophecy for believers in Jesus Christ. We now have Immanuel, God with us, by His indwelling Spirit. He is our salvation! He is strong enough to have overcome sin and death inherent in our world since the Genesis 3 fall, resurrected in that strength.

"In the world you will have tribulation. But take heart; I have overcome the world" (Jn. 16:33). Because God is strong, because nothing is too hard for Him, we can trust His strengthening work in our suffering too. By His Spirit, ours because of the work of the gospel (Eph. 1:3-14), He provides strength for us to walk through suffering with joy (Neh. 8:10). Beloved, let's praise Him for His strength today and discover more about how His strength affects us as we suffer.

What do you re-discover about God's strength in these verses?

Exodus 15:2

1 Chronicles 16:11

Isaiah 12:2

Ephesians 3:16

Ephesians 6:10-13

My prayer-song to You, my Strong Lord:

IN MY SUFFERING, YOU SAY THIS IS TRUE:

SO, IN MY SUFFERING, I PRAISE YOU BECAUSE:

IN MY SUFFERING, PLEASE HELP ME WITH:

INTO MY SUFFERING, I'LL SING THESE SONGS FROM MY PLAYLIST TO YOU TODAY:

Who trusts in God, a strong abode
in heav'n and earth possesses;
who looks in love to Christ above,
no fear his heart oppresses.
In you alone, dear Lord, we own
sweet hope and consolation;
our shield from foes, our balm for woes,
our great and sure salvation.

Though Satan's wrath beset our path,
and worldly scorn assail us,
while you are near we will not fear,
your strength shall never fail us:
your rod and staff shall keep us safe,
and guide our steps forever;
nor shades of death, nor hell beneath,
our souls from you shall sever.

In all the strife of mortal life
our feet shall stand securely;
temptation's hour shall lose its pow'r,
for you shall guard us surely.
O God, renew, with heav'nly dew,
our body, soul, and spirit,
until we stand at your right hand,
through Jesus' saving merit.

("WHO TRUSTS IN GOD, A STRONG ABODE," MAGDEBURG, J., 1572, ANON.,
1597)

♪ ♪ ♪

DAY 21: COMPASSIONATE AND MERCIFUL

*A*s one who suffers with chronic illness, the Lord's compassion and mercy often rise to the front of my prayers. Sometimes it feels Job-like when suffering doesn't go away. The Lord's compassion and mercy held His purposes for Job, in the suffering. His compassionate mercy envelopes ours as well and He considers us blessed when we remain steadfast in our suffering like Job (Jas. 5:11).

In Scripture, God's mercy is tender, affectionate, cherishing. He pities us in our need. It's wrapped in our Father's deep love for us as His believing children. Sisters, if you've experienced a baby's hunger cries, you know it's compassion that literally sustains their lives despite our weariness in constant feedings. "Can a woman forget her nursing child, that she should have no compassion on the son of her womb? Even these may forget, yet I will not forget you" (Is. 49:15).

How is His mercy revealed to us, in today's pain? It began when He drew us to Jesus and brought us into new life, washing and saving us. "Blessed be the God and Father of our Lord Jesus Christ! According to his great *mercy*, he has caused us to be born again to a living hope through the resurrection of Jesus Christ from the dead" (1 Pet. 1:3, emphasis added). "He saved us, not because of works done by us in righteousness, but according to his own *mercy*, by the washing of regeneration and renewal of the Holy Spirit" (Ti. 3:5, emphasis added).

Beloved, it begins there, because He made you His child and your Father will never forget you. "I have engraved you on the palms of my hands; your walls are continually before me" (Is. 49:16). In His compassion, He has not forgotten you in today's pain.

Consider Jesus, whose pity and compassion fueled His miracles (e.g., Mt. 14:14; 20:34; Lk. 7:13). Jesus didn't perform a miracle for everyone He met, but He knew each physical, emotional, and spiritual need. He knew what they needed most. So, our unchanging and compassionate Lord knows our biggest needs now. In His perfect wisdom, He knows better than we do. Beloved, "let us then with confidence draw near to the throne of grace, so that we may receive mercy and find grace to help in time of need" (Heb. 4:16).

What do you re-discover about God's merciful compassion in these verses?

EPHESIANS 2:4-9

LUKE 15:18-24

DEUTERONOMY 4:29-31

ISAIAH 49:13

71

My prayer-song to You, merciful and compassionate God:

IN MY SUFFERING, YOU SAY THIS IS TRUE:

SO, IN MY SUFFERING, I PRAISE YOU BECAUSE:

IN MY SUFFERING, PLEASE HELP ME WITH:

INTO MY SUFFERING, I'LL SING THESE SONGS FROM MY PLAYLIST TO YOU TODAY:

When all your mercies, O my God,
my rising soul surveys,
transported with the view, I'm lost
in wonder, love, and praise.

Unnumbered comforts to my soul
your tender care bestowed,
before my infant heart conceived
from whom those comforts flowed.

When worn with sickness, oft have you
with health renewed my face;
and when in sins and sorrows sunk,
revived my soul with grace.

Ten thousand thousand precious gifts
my daily thanks employ;
nor is the least a cheerful heart
that tastes those gifts with joy.

Through ev'ry period of my life
your goodness I'll pursue;
and after death, in distant worlds,
the glorious theme renew.

Through all eternity to you
a joyful song I'll raise;
for oh, eternity's too short
to utter all your praise.

("WHEN ALL THY MERCIES, O MY GOD," ADDISON, J., 1727)

♪ ♪ ♪

DAY 22: PROVIDER

Can you imagine Abraham's anguish? God had told him to kill his beloved son, offering him as a burnt offering. "Where is the lamb, Daddy?" Abraham believed, "God will provide for himself the lamb" and indeed, God did. God had promised that He'd create a people for Himself through Abraham's family. How could that happen if Isaac were dead? After forty years of Abraham's bumpy faith journey, God tested Abraham's trust in His promised provision, even when Abraham couldn't figure out how (Gen. 22:1-14). It was a test of Abraham's reverent fear of the Lord, above all he could see right now.

We often can't understand either. Because sometimes, we don't see God's provision of answered prayer today. And yet, God promises He is our all-sufficient provider today and every future day. "God will supply every need of yours according to his riches in glory in Christ Jesus" (Phil. 4:19).

Our compassionate, wise, good, and powerful God knows our needs, and promises to abundantly provide those needs. What are they? Perhaps we actually need joy, thanksgiving, and peace when we're anxious (Phil. 4:4-7).

Sometimes our needs are for material things like food and clothes. Jesus promises, "Your heavenly Father knows that you need them all"

(Mt. 6:32). Because God is always good, always righteous, always wise, always loving, and sovereign over all, we can trust that He always gives us what we are really needing.

Perhaps what we need most is contentment with God's provision. "I have learned in whatever situation I am to be content. I know how to be brought low, and I know how to *abound* in every circumstance... I can do all things through him who strengthens me" (Phil. 4:11-13, emphasis added).

Back to Abraham, for a moment. God enabled Abraham to trust in His provision. Because God is God, Abraham could endure his current pain with faith in how God would provide in His perfect way. "He considered that God was able even to raise [Isaac] from the dead" (Heb. 11:17-19). Abraham "grew strong in his faith *as he gave glory to God*, fully convinced that God was able to do what he had promised" (Rom. 4:20, emphasis added). God promises to supply our needs too, because He knows what is best for us, His beloved children. Let's give glory to God too!

What do you re-discover about God as provider in these verses?

ISAIAH 41:10

1 CORINTHIANS 10:13-14

GALATIANS 3:29

EPHESIANS 1:11-14

My prayer-song to You, my providing Lord:

IN MY SUFFERING, YOU SAY THIS IS TRUE:

SO, IN MY SUFFERING, I PRAISE YOU BECAUSE:

IN MY SUFFERING, PLEASE HELP ME WITH:

INTO MY SUFFERING, I'LL SING THESE SONGS FROM MY PLAYLIST TO YOU TODAY:

Be not dismayed whate'er betide,
God will take care of you;
beneath his wings of love abide,
God will take care of you.

Through days of toil when heart doth fail,
God will take care of you;
when dangers fierce your path assail,
God will take care of you.

All you may need he will provide,
God will take care of you;
trust him and you will be satisfied,
God will take care of you.

No matter what may be the test,
God will take care of you;
lean, weary one, upon his breast,
God will take care of you.

God will take care of you,
through ev'ry day, o'er all the way;
he will take care of you,
God will take care of you.

("GOD WILL TAKE CARE OF YOU," MARTIN, C. D., 1904)

♪ ♪ ♪

DAY 23: PATIENT

I love the original Hebrew word for patient…"longsuffering." Are you suffering long today? Has suffering been a part of most of your life? Perhaps God's patience is your cling-to character attribute today. Maybe you're praying for your own patience in spite of troubles, in the midst of trouble. Let's consider His patience to fuel our own!

Another common Biblical definition for patient is "slow to anger" (e.g., Ps. 86:15; I Pet. 3:9). When God rewrote His commandments for Moses after His sinful people violated them, Moses responded in worship (Ex. 34:8). Perhaps Moses understood that God is patient with us because He *is* patient, praising "a God merciful and gracious, slow to anger, and abounding in steadfast love and faithfulness" (Ex. 34:6).

In God's case, He is so patient with His beloved children that He gave Jesus to us. Not only is He slow to anger, but He actually removed His righteous wrath for those who are in Christ. "For God has not destined us for wrath, but to obtain salvation through our Lord Jesus Christ" (1 Thess. 5:9).

Could your current life of longsuffering be a special ministry to those who don't know Jesus as Lord? "I received mercy for this reason, that in me…Jesus Christ might display his perfect patience as an example to those who were to believe in him for eternal life" (1 Tim. 1:16). As we suffer, why has He kept us here instead of bringing us to our eternal home with Him forever?

When I'm impatient with my suffering, I continually must remember that "with the Lord one day is as a thousand years, and a thousand years as one day" (2 Pet. 3:15). His timing is different than ours, His waiting has purpose, and His patience means salvation.

"The Lord is not slow to fulfill his promise as some count slowness, but is patient toward you, not wishing that any should perish, but that all should reach *repentance*" (2 Pet. 3:9, emphasis added). Could God's patience be on display in your own suffering as part of His kingdom work, as a witness of gospel hope to others who need redemption? "There is joy before the angels of God over one sinner who repents" (Lk. 15:10). Let's ask our patient, longsuffering, slow to anger God for His Spirit's help to rightly respond to our suffering with active patience, as we seek the kingdom work He's doing in us, through it all. Beloved, our long-suffering God is holding us fast in our suffering.

What do you re-discover about your response to God's patience in these verses?

PSALM 40:1-5

ROMANS 12:12

GALATIANS 5:22-23

JAMES 5:7-11

My prayer-song to You, my Patient Father:

IN MY SUFFERING, YOU SAY THIS IS TRUE:

SO, IN MY SUFFERING, I PRAISE YOU BECAUSE:

IN MY SUFFERING, PLEASE HELP ME WITH:

INTO MY SUFFERING, I'LL SING THESE SONGS FROM MY PLAYLIST TO YOU TODAY:

When I fear my faith will fail,
Christ will hold me fast;
When the tempter would prevail,
He can hold me fast!

I could never keep my hold,
He must hold me fast;
For my love is often cold,
He must hold me fast.

I am precious in His sight,
He will hold me fast;
Those He saves are His delight,
He will hold me fast.

He'll not let my soul be lost,
Christ will hold me fast;
Bought by Him at such a cost,
He will hold me fast.

He will hold me fast,
He will hold me fast;
For my Savior loves me so,
He will hold me fast.

("HE WILL HOLD ME FAST," HABERSHON, A. R., 1908)

♪ ♪ ♪

Near the cross I'll watch and wait,
Hoping, trusting ever,
Till I reach the golden strand
just beyond the river.

("JESUS, KEEP ME NEAR THE CROSS," CROSBY, F. J., 1869)

DAY 24: I AM, ALPHA AND OMEGA

*W*hen suffering overwhelms me, I must remember how big God is. Because He is I AM, God is self-existent, constant, and always accomplishes His purposes. He has always existed outside of what we perceive as time, space, location. Anything that exists is because God *is*...and He always will be. Let's remember together, beloved. Like the Psalmist praying in lament of trouble, let's turn around to our great I AM, to interrupt our suffering. I'm suffering today...

"*But* you, O LORD, are enthroned forever; you are remembered throughout all generations" (Ps. 102:12, emphasis added).

Let's remember, resetting our thoughts about God. First, the beginning! In His always and forever self-existence..."In the beginning, God created the heavens and the earth" (Gen. 1:1). God, Father, Son, Holy Spirit, in His glorious trinitarian self-existence made everything we see and experience, by His Word. Remember the grandeur... Jesus was the Word.

"In the beginning was the Word, and the Word was with God, and the Word was God. He was in the beginning with God. All things were made through him, and without him was not any thing made that was made" (Jn. 1:1-3).

Then, the present! Let's remember that our resurrected and self-existent Jesus is right now seated on His throne, sustaining all things. "He is the image of the invisible God, the firstborn of all creation. For by him all things were created, in heaven and on earth, visible and invisible, whether thrones or dominions or rulers or authorities—all things were created through him and for him. And he is before all things, and in him all things hold together" (Col. 1:15-17).

Then, what's to come! Let's have hope in the promises of our Alpha and Omega for the future. "But according to his promise we are waiting for new heavens and a new earth in which righteousness dwells" (2 Pet. 3:13).

What do you re-discover about God's self-existence in these verses?

Revelation 1:8

John 8:58

Psalm 46:1-11

Isaiah 30:15

My prayer-song to You, Alpha and Omega, I AM:

IN MY SUFFERING, YOU SAY THIS IS TRUE:

SO, IN MY SUFFERING, I PRAISE YOU BECAUSE:

IN MY SUFFERING, PLEASE HELP ME WITH:

INTO MY SUFFERING, I'LL SING THESE SONGS FROM MY PLAYLIST TO YOU TODAY:

Of the Father's love begotten
ere the worlds began to be,
he is Alpha and Omega,
he the Source, the Ending he,
of the things that are, that have been,
and that future years shall see,
evermore and evermore!

This is he whom heav'n-taught singers
sang of old with one accord,
whom the Scriptures of the prophets
promised in their faithful word;
now he shines, the long-expected;
let creation praise its Lord,
evermore and evermore!

O ye heights of heav'n, adore him;
angel hosts, his praises sing;
all dominions, bow before him,
and extol our God and King;
let no tongue on earth be silent,
ev'ry voice in concert ring,
evermore and evermore!

Christ, to thee, with God the Father,
and, O Holy Ghost, to thee,
hymn, and chant, and high thanksgiving,
and unwearied praises be,
honor, glory, and dominion,
and eternal victory,
evermore and evermore!

("OF THE FATHER'S LOVE BEGOTTEN," PRUDENTIUS, A. C., TRANS. BAKER &
NEALE, PUBLIC DOMAIN)

DAY 25: ETERNAL AND EVERLASTING

*G*od's self-existence means He is everlasting, infinite, eternal. Beloved, this means all aspects of His character are eternal and everlasting, revealed to us in His Word.

"Before the mountains were brought forth, or ever you had formed the earth and the world, from everlasting to everlasting you are God" (Ps. 90:2). "The eternal God is your dwelling place, and underneath are the everlasting arms" (Deut. 33:27a).

What does He show us about Jesus Christ as eternal and everlasting? "And to him was given dominion and glory and a kingdom, that all peoples, nations, and languages should serve him. His dominion is an *everlasting* dominion, which shall not pass away, and his kingdom will not be destroyed" (Dan. 7:14, emphasis added).

In our suffering, we can know that God's promises to a believer in Jesus Christ are everlasting, because God *is* everlasting. Lasting forever, eternally. In all of the global suffering we experience today.

By His grace and through the gospel, "as many as were appointed to eternal life believed" (Acts 13:48). Eternal life is our promise and it's assured because it is a gift from Him (Jn. 3:16-18, 36; 5:24; 6:40; 10:28; 17:1-3). So, we have everlasting "hope of eternal life, which God, who never lies, promised before the ages began" (Ti 1:2).

As we suffer on earth and wait for this hope to be fulfilled, we also have His always-lasting promises, such as: "And God is able to make *all* grace abound to you, so that having *all* sufficiency in *all* things at *all* times, you may abound in *every* good work" (2 Cor. 9:6, emphasis added). "The LORD is the everlasting God, the Creator of the ends of the earth. He does not faint or grow weary; his understanding is unsearchable" (Is. 40:28). Hallelujah!

What do you re-discover about our eternal God in these verses?

1 JOHN 5:11-12

2 THESSALONIANS 2:13-16

PSALM 106:48

1 TIMOTHY 1:17

My prayer-song to You, my eternal and everlasting Lord:

IN MY SUFFERING, YOU SAY THIS IS TRUE:

SO, IN MY SUFFERING, I PRAISE YOU BECAUSE:

IN MY SUFFERING, PLEASE HELP ME WITH:

INTO MY SUFFERING, I'LL SING THESE SONGS FROM MY PLAYLIST TO YOU TODAY:

Our God, our help in ages past,
our hope for years to come,
our shelter from the stormy blast,
and our eternal home:

Under the shadow of your throne
your saints have dwelt secure;
sufficient is your arm alone,
and our defense is sure.

Before the hills in order stood,
or earth received her frame,
from everlasting you are God,
to endless years the same.

(*"OUR GOD, OUR HELP IN AGES PAST," WATTS, I., 1719*)

♪ ♪ ♪

Neither life nor death shall ever
from the Lord his children sever;
unto them his grace he showeth,
and their sorrows all he knoweth.

More secure is no one ever
than the loved ones of the Savior;
not yon star on high abiding
nor the bird in home-nest hiding.

Praise the Lord in joyful numbers,
your Protector never slumbers;
at the will of your Defender
ev'ry foeman must surrender.

(*"CHILDREN OF THE HEAVENLY FATHER," SANDELL BERG, C., 1855*)

DAY 26: COMFORTER AND HELPER

*I*n my suffering, many prayers are often simply, "Help me." He answers that prayer continually. God is our Helper and Comforter, in the person of the Holy Spirit. What a gift!

Jesus told His disciples, "And I will ask the Father, and he will give you another Helper, to be with you forever, even the Spirit of truth, whom the world cannot receive, because it neither sees him nor knows him. You know him, for he dwells with you and will be in you" (Jn. 14:16-17).

He helps us believe in moments of fear and doubt (Mk. 9:24). Because Jesus suffered temptations and trials in this fallen world of sin, yet lived a totally sinless life, "he is able to help those who are being tempted" as we endure trials (Heb. 2:18). "Even though I walk through the valley of the shadow of death, I will fear no evil, for you are with me, your rod and your staff, they comfort me" (Ps. 23:4).

By His Spirit's indwelling presence, illuminating His Word to our hearts, He protects and guides our hearts and thoughts. The Holy Spirit convicts, teaches, refreshes, and leads us when we forget. He helps us remember His Word (Jn. 14:26). According to Isaiah 51, it's in the "waste places," "wilderness," "devastation and destruction, famine and sword" that we forget. It's when we're "bowed down," poured out, feeling afraid of others and what's happening to us. It's when we're afflicted that He comforts and helps us.

"I, I am he who comforts you...I have put my words in your mouth and covered you in the shadow of my hand" (Is. 51:12, 16). "Blessed are those who mourn, for they shall be comforted" (Mt. 5:4).

What do you re-discover about God's help and comfort in these verses?

PSALM 118:6-9

2 CORINTHIANS 1:3-5

EPHESIANS 3:16

My prayer-song to You, my comforter and helper:

IN MY SUFFERING, YOU SAY THIS IS TRUE:

SO, IN MY SUFFERING, I PRAISE YOU BECAUSE:

IN MY SUFFERING, PLEASE HELP ME WITH:

INTO MY SUFFERING, I'LL SING THESE SONGS FROM MY PLAYLIST TO YOU TODAY:

Spirit of God, descend upon my heart;
wean it from earth, through all its pulses move;
stoop to my weakness, mighty as thou art,
and make me love thee as I ought to love.

I ask no dream, no prophet ecstasies,
no sudden rending of the veil of clay,
no angel visitant, no op'ning skies;
but take the dimness of my soul away.

Hast thou not bid us love thee, God and King?
All, all thine own, soul, heart, and strength and mind.
I see the cross– there teach my heart to cling:
O let me seek thee, and O let me find.

Teach me to feel that thou art always nigh;
teach me the struggles of the soul to bear,
to check the rising doubt, the rebel sigh;
teach me the patience of unanswered prayer.

("SPIRIT OF GOD, DESCEND UPON MY HEART," CROLY, G., *1854*)

♪ ♪ ♪

The Lord's my Shepherd, I'll not want;
he makes me down to lie
in pastures green; he leadeth me
the quiet waters by.
Yea, though I walk in death's dark vale,
yet will I fear none ill,
for thou art with me; and thy rod
and staff me comfort still.

("THE LORD'S MY SHEPHERD, I'LL NOT WANT," ROUS, F. ET AL., *1650*)

DAY 27: FATHER

Our beloved Savior says, "Pray then like this: '*Our Father* in heaven, hallowed be your name'" (Mt. 6:9, emphasis added).

We "hallow" God, acknowledging that He is the Lord, holy and set apart, pure and sacred. We pray that others would acknowledge who He is. For we who are "in Christ," He is our heavenly Father.

"I will be a father to you, and you shall be sons and daughters to me, says the Lord Almighty" (2 Cor. 6:18).

We come back to his perfect, set apart, holy *hesed* love today, because sometimes, earthly fathers have hurt us and it's hard to even see the word "Father." Beloved, if this is you, know that the love of your heavenly Father is always good, wise, and kind. There is no sin in God, unlike every single earthly father.

"See what kind of love the Father has given to us, that we should be called children of God" (1 Jn. 3:1). In His uniquely perfect love as our Father, we no longer need to fear Him in terror and dread. Through Jesus, we have an intimate and close relationship with our Father. He's gifted us with His permanent love, even when we sin (1 Jn. 2:1). "God has sent the Spirit of his Son into our hearts, crying 'Abba! Father!'" (Gal. 4:6).

Even when we're suffering. Consider that our "older brother" (that would be Jesus, according to Rom. 8:29!) suffered far worse than we ever could (Heb. 2:10-13). Remember that our perfect and unchanging Father gives good gifts to us...even as we suffer (Mt. 7:9-11; Jas. 1:17). And one day? Each child of God is a fellow heir with Jesus! Let's pray with hope as we wait to see Him in our glorious inheritance. Let's rest with our heavenly Father of love in today's suffering, beloved in Christ.

What do you re-discover about your Father in these verses?

JOHN 14:1-4

ROMANS 8:15-17

EPHESIANS 3:17-19

REVELATION 3:5

My prayer-song to You, my Father in heaven:

IN MY SUFFERING, YOU SAY THIS IS TRUE:

SO, IN MY SUFFERING, I PRAISE YOU BECAUSE:

IN MY SUFFERING, PLEASE HELP ME WITH:

INTO MY SUFFERING, I'LL SING THESE SONGS FROM MY PLAYLIST TO YOU TODAY:

Children of the heav'nly Father
safely in his bosom gather;
nestling bird nor star in heaven
such a refuge e'er was given.

Though he giveth or he taketh,
God his children ne'er forsaketh;
his the loving purpose solely
to preserve them pure and holy.

("CHILDREN OF THE HEAVENLY FATHER," SANDELL BERG, C., 1855)

♪ ♪ ♪

My Father is rich in houses and lands,
he holdeth the wealth of the world in his hands!
Of rubies and diamonds, of silver and gold,
his coffers are full, he has riches untold.

My Father's own Son, the Savior of men,
once wandered on earth as the poorest of them;
but now he is reigning forever on high,
and will give me a home in heav'n by and by.

I once was an outcast stranger on earth,
a sinner by choice, an alien by birth!
But I've been adopted, my name's written down,
an heir to a mansion, a robe and a crown.

A tent or a cottage, why should I care?
They're building a palace for me over there!
Though exiled from home, yet still may I sing:
all glory to God, I'm a child of the King.
With Jesus, my Savior, I'm a child of the King.

("A CHILD OF THE KING," BUELL, H. E., 1877)

DAY 28: SAVIOR

$\mathcal{W}$e cherish God as Savior, don't we? That name became even more precious to me when I discovered that the Hebrew for "save" means He makes open, wide, free, safe, delivered from evil. Nothing and no one else can save us from evil except God (Is. 43:11; Hos. 13:4). We expect manmade institutions to do so, but saving is God's doing. He's saving us now, even as we suffer.

Imagine the joy! "For unto you is born...a Savior, who is Christ the Lord" (Lk. 2:11). With Messianic prophecies fulfilled, God came to earth as Jesus, our deliverer. "There is salvation in no one else, for there is no other name under heaven given among men by which we must be saved" (Acts 4:12).

In the Greek, God "saves" us by rescuing, keeping us safe from destruction, healing and making us whole. What are we saved from? Separation from God and His righteous wrath for our sin. We were all born "dead in the trespasses and sins...the course of this world...at work in the sons of disobedience...by nature children of wrath, like the rest of mankind" (Eph. 2:1-3). But our merciful and loving God *saved* us, making us alive in Christ and with Christ (Eph. 2:4-6)! The gospel "by which you are being saved" (1 Cor. 15:2) gives us resurrection hope beyond this life (1 Cor. 15:19).

So, what are we saved for? What is our hope now? God's transforming us to become more like Jesus, giving us good works to do (Ti. 2:14). What a comfort that "[Jesus] is able to save to the uttermost those who draw near to God through him, since he always lives to make intercession for them" (Heb. 7:25). Jesus is praying for us. As you suffer today, what is our Savior showing you in this Scripture? "That I may know him and the power of his resurrection, and may share his sufferings, becoming like him in his death" (Phil. 3:10).

What do you re-discover about your Savior in these verses?

JOHN 10:9, 14-15

2 PETER 3:18

1 JOHN 4:17-18

JUDE 24-25

My prayer-song to You, my Savior:

IN MY SUFFERING, YOU SAY THIS IS TRUE:

SO, IN MY SUFFERING, I PRAISE YOU BECAUSE:

IN MY SUFFERING, PLEASE HELP ME WITH:

INTO MY SUFFERING, I'LL SING THESE SONGS FROM MY PLAYLIST TO YOU TODAY:

My Jesus, I love thee, I know thou art mine;
for thee all the follies of sin I resign.
My gracious Redeemer, my Savior art thou;
If ever I loved thee, my Jesus, 'tis now.

I love thee because thou hast first loved me,
and purchased my pardon on Calvary's tree.
I love thee for wearing the thorns on thy brow;
if ever I loved thee, my Jesus, 'tis now.

I'll love thee in life, I will love thee in death;
and praise thee as long as thou lendest me breath;
and say, when the death-dew lies cold on my brow:
if ever I loved thee, my Jesus, 'tis now.

In mansions of glory and endless delight,
I'll ever adore thee in heaven so bright;
I'll sing with the glittering crown on my brow:
if ever I loved thee, my Jesus, 'tis now.

("MY JESUS, I LOVE THEE," FEATHERSTON, W. R., 1862)

♪ ♪ ♪

I'm so glad I learned to trust thee,
Precious Jesus, Savior, Friend;
And I know that thou art with me,
Wilt be with me to the end.
Jesus, Jesus, how I trust him!
How I've proved him o'er and o'er!
Jesus, Jesus, precious Jesus!
O for grace to trust him more!

("'TIS SO SWEET TO TRUST IN JESUS," STEAD, L. M. R., 1882)

DAY 29: HOPE

*H*ope keeps us going in our suffering. It's our look to the future in order to endure the present. So what is our hope, as Christians? Is it that our suffering will end while we live on earth? Oh, let's pray for it, knowing that our powerful and sovereign God can and often does ease our suffering in earthly life. But He tells us to "set your hope *fully* on the grace that will be brought to you *at the revelation of Jesus Christ*" (1 Pet. 1:13, emphasis added).

We have all hope! By grace, Christ came and saved us, He's sanctifying us now and we're "waiting for our blessed hope, the appearing of the glory of our great God and Savior Jesus Christ" (Ti. 2:13). God's glorious character, revealed in Jesus in His first coming, is our hope as we wait for His second coming.

One day, only His believing children will live with Him for all eternity, in the new heavens and earth (Rev. 21). All that we currently know and see will be destroyed by God, in His righteous and just wrath for sin. "But our citizenship is in heaven, and from it we await a Savior, the Lord Jesus Christ, who will transform our lowly body to be like his glorious body, by the power that enables him even to subject all things to himself" (Phil. 3:20-21).

As we await our Savior and suffer in this fallen world, we groan along with His whole creation, affected by sin since Genesis 3. Our pain drives us to hope in Christ and the day sin and evil will no longer exist. "For in this hope we were saved...if we hope for what we do not see, we wait for it with patience" (Rom. 8:22-25).

"So we do not lose heart. Though our outer self is wasting away, our inner self is being renewed day by day. For this light momentary affliction is preparing for us an eternal weight of glory beyond all comparison, as we look not to the things that are seen but to the things that are unseen. For the things that are seen are transient, but the things that are unseen are eternal" (2 Cor. 4:16-18).

What do you re-discover about hope in who God is, in these verses?

PSALM 42:5

PSALM 119:81

1 THESSALONIANS 5:8-11

REVELATION 21:1-7

My prayer-song to You, my Hope:

IN MY SUFFERING, YOU SAY THIS IS TRUE:

SO, IN MY SUFFERING, I PRAISE YOU BECAUSE:

IN MY SUFFERING, PLEASE HELP ME WITH:

INTO MY SUFFERING, I'LL SING THESE SONGS FROM MY PLAYLIST TO YOU TODAY:

His oath, his covenant, his blood
support me in the whelming flood;
when all around my soul gives way,
he then is all my hope and stay.

When he shall come with trumpet sound,
O may I then in him be found;
dressed in his righteousness alone,
faultless to stand before the throne.

On Christ, the solid rock, I stand;
all other ground is sinking sand.

("My Hope is Built on Nothing Less," Note, E., 1834)

♪ ♪ ♪

Our God, our help in ages past,
our hope for years to come,
our shelter from the stormy blast,
and our eternal home:

Under the shadow of your throne
your saints have dwelt secure;
sufficient is your arm alone,
and our defense is sure.

Before the hills in order stood,
or earth received her frame,
from everlasting you are God,
to endless years the same.

("O God, Our Help in Ages Past," Watts, I., 1719)

DAY 30: WORTHY OF PRAISE

So, we don't lose heart! Our Triune God has given us Scripture about Himself to keep us from despair and hopelessness as we walk through this fallen world's deep suffering. When suffering lingers, we battle the enemy's insidious lies just as Jesus did; we battle with the Word of God and its truths about who God *is* and therefore, what He *does* from His unchanging character. We are near to God and He is so near to us.

In realizing His gracious gift to us in Christ, we who are so unworthy fall before the only One who is praiseworthy. In the hard, human days of emotional lament, it can be hard to praise God as Scriptural laments do. How can we find the words? *"Through him* then let us continually offer up a sacrifice of praise to God, that is, the fruit of lips that acknowledge his name" (Heb. 13:15, emphasis added). Here are some Scriptures to pray in those moments, for the Lord is worthy, beloved in Christ.

"Yours, O LORD, is the greatness and the power and the glory and the victory and the majesty, for all that is in the heavens and in the earth is yours. Yours is the kingdom, O LORD, and you are exalted as head above all" (I Chron. 29:11).

"Worthy are you, our Lord and God, to receive glory and honor and power, for you created all things, and by your will they existed and were created" (Rev. 4:11).

"Worthy are you to take the scroll and to open its seals, for you were slain, and by your blood you ransomed people for God from every tribe and language and people and nation" (Rev. 5:9).

"Praise the LORD! Oh give thanks to the LORD, for he is good, for his steadfast love endures forever!" (Ps. 106:1)

"I will bless the LORD at all times; his praise shall continually be in my mouth" (Ps. 34:1).

"Praise the LORD! For it is good to sing praises to our God; for it is pleasant, and a song of praise is fitting" (Ps. 147:1).

May God draw us nearer to Himself, every day of our suffering on earth, until we one day sing these words to His face, for eternity!

What do you re-discover about God's praiseworthiness in these verses?

REVELATION 5:12

PSALM 145

My prayer-song to You, my praiseworthy Lord:

IN MY SUFFERING, YOU SAY THIS IS TRUE:

SO, IN MY SUFFERING, I PRAISE YOU BECAUSE:

IN MY SUFFERING, PLEASE HELP ME WITH:

INTO MY SUFFERING, I'LL SING THESE SONGS FROM MY PLAYLIST TO YOU TODAY:

O worship the King all glorious above,
O gratefully sing his pow'r and his love;
Our Shield and Defender, the Ancient of Days,
Pavilioned in splendor, and girded with praise.

Frail children of dust, and feeble as frail,
In thee do we trust, nor find thee to fail;
Thy mercies how tender, how firm to the end,
Our Maker, Defender, Redeemer, and Friend!

O measureless Might! Ineffable Love!
While angels delight to hymn thee above,
The humbler creation, though feeble their lays,
With true adoration shall lisp to thy praise.

("O Worship the King," Grant, R., 1833)

♪ ♪ ♪

All praise to God, who reigns above,
the God of all creation,
the God of wonders, pow'r, and love,
the God of our salvation!
With healing balm my soul he fills,
the God who every sorrow stills.
To God all praise and glory!
I cried to him in time of need:
Lord God, O hear my calling!
For death he gave me life indeed
and kept my feet from falling.
For this my thanks shall endless be;
O thank him, thank our God, with me.
To God all praise and glory!

("All Praise to God, Who Reigns Above," Schütz, J. J., Trans. Cox, F.
E., 1675)

SOME AFTER THOUGHTS

First, thank you so much for reading this book. I've prayed it would be the Lord's blessing to you as you walk through this difficult time.

As you may know, many people read **Amazon reviews** before they decide to read a book. Could you please take a minute to review this book and share some honest feedback with me and others? It would help me in creating future projects. This is my first!

Second, I am creating **weekly playlist gifts** of Psalms, hymns, and spiritual songs to coordinate with each of these aspects of God's character. They're for our use in personal worship time, as praise-filled prayer responses to the Lord. If you would like to receive them in your email each week, contact me at my website.

Third, this is my deepest **prayer for you**, fellow sufferer. "May the God of hope fill you with all joy and peace in believing, so that by the power of the Holy Spirit you may abound in hope" (Rom. 15:13).

In Christ,
Lauri

ABOUT THE AUTHOR

Dr. Lauri Hogle's journey of suffering interweaves with her lifelong passion to glorify God through music, teaching, research, and writing. As a church music/children's/women's ministry leader, music educator, music therapist, research scholar, and author, her words and musical offerings have touched lives across the globe. She is the founder of Singing Christ's Hope, a nonprofit ministry for Christian women who are walking through suffering. Although she has been a prolific academic writer and active speaker and teacher, her greatest joy is as wife, mother, and Nana. God's sweet gifts of grace include continual stacks of books, coffee, knitting, candles, and beautiful foretastes of eternal song.

You can find and contact Lauri at www.laurihogle.com.